# THE
# GREAT DANE

by Charlotte Wilcox

*Content Consultant*
Sandy Lady
President
Great Dane Club of America

## CAPSTONE PRESS
### MANKATO, MINNESOTA

# C A P S T O N E   P R E S S

818 North Willow Street • Mankato, MN 56001
http://www.capstone-press.com

Printed in the United States of America.

*Library of Congress Cataloging-in-Publication Data*
Wilcox, Charlotte.
    The Great Dane/by Charlotte Wilcox.
    p. cm.--(Learning about dogs)
    Includes bibliographical references (p. 45) and index.
    Summary: Discusses the history, physical characteristics, care, and breeding of this dog, one of the largest breeds in the world.
    ISBN 1-56065-543-7
    1. Great Danes--Juvenile literature. [1. Great Danes. 2. Dogs.]
I. Title. II. Series: Wilcox, Charlotte.  Learning about dogs.
SF429.G7W55  1998
636.73--dc21

                                    97-13113
                                      CIP
                                       AC

Photo credits
Maguire PhotoGraFX, 37
Mark Raycroft, cover, 4, 8, 12, 17, 24, 34, 40-41
Unicorn/Betts Anderson, 6, 26, 31, 32; Rob Furgason, 21,
    28; Ed Harp, 38
Faith A. Uridel, 18, 22
Visuals Unlimited/Warren Stone, 10, 14

# Table of Contents

## *Quick Facts about the Great Dane*

### Description

Height:    Male Great Danes stand 30 to 36 inches
(76 to 91 centimeters) tall. Females
stand 28 to 34 inches (71 to 86
centimeters) tall or taller. Height is
measured from the ground to the
withers. The withers are the tops of the
shoulders.

Weight:    Males weigh 140 to 175 pounds (63 to
79 kilograms). Females weigh 110 to
140 pounds (49.5 to 63 kilograms).

| Physical features: | Great Danes are giant dogs. Their heads are large and square. Their tails are long and curved. Their coats are short and smooth. |
|---|---|
| Color: | Great Danes are usually fawn, brindle, blue, harlequin, or mantle. Fawn is gold with a black face. Brindle is gold with black, tiger-like stripes and a black face. Blue is steel gray. Harlequin is white with black markings all over the body except the neck. Mantle is a black body with a white neck and front. Danes can also be white and merle, but these colors are not used for breeding. Merle is speckled gray. |

## Development

| Place of origin: | Great Danes were developed in Germany. |
|---|---|
| History of breed: | Danes descended from mastiffs. These are large, ancient hunting dogs from Asia. |
| Numbers: | About 11,000 Great Danes are registered every year in the United States. Register means to record a dog's breeding records with an official club. About 700 Danes are registered each year in Canada. |

## Uses

Most Great Danes in North America are family pets. A few are service dogs for people with disabilities.

# Chapter 1

# The Gentle Giant

Millions of people know at least one Great Dane. His tricks are reported in newspapers every day. More than 25 books have been written about him. His name is Marmaduke. He is the most famous Great Dane in the world.

Marmaduke is a comic-strip character. He was created in 1954 by cartoonist Brad Anderson. He remains a favorite cartoon dog year after year. Marmaduke introduced millions of people to the lovable, playful Great Dane.

**Great Danes are lovable, playful dogs.**

## One of the Largest Dogs

Many people think the Great Dane came from Denmark. This is because a person from Denmark is called a Dane. But Great Danes were developed in Germany.

The Great Dane is one of the largest dog breeds in the world. Danes weigh as much as a grown man. They are taller than some ponies. They can measure almost six feet (almost two meters) from the nose to the tip of the tail.

They are big in other ways, too. They have big hearts. Great Danes will show love for their human families. They are kind dogs that seem aware of others' feelings. But these gentle giants were once trained to kill wild animals.

**Great Danes are among the largest dogs in the world.**

# Chapter 2

# The Beginnings of the Breed

Great Danes came from an ancient hunting dog called the mastiff. Mastiffs were used for thousands of years in Asia, Africa, and Europe. Pictures of mastiffs were found on 3,000-year-old Egyptian monuments. The oldest written description of a mastiff was found in Chinese literature.

People in the ancient Middle East and Africa used mastiffs. They hunted lions, bulls, and wild donkeys with the dogs. Europeans used them, too. In Europe, they were used to hunt bears, wolves, and boars. A boar is a wild pig.

**Great Danes came from an ancient dog called the mastiff.**

**Great Danes are called Deutsche dogges in Germany. This means German mastiffs.**

Many breeds came from the ancient mastiff. Some of the oldest are the Irish wolfhound and the English mastiff. These breeds were well known in Europe more than 1,000 years ago.

## Hunting the Wild Boar

The modern Great Dane first appeared in Germany about 400 years ago. It was probably a cross between the Irish wolfhound and the English mastiff. It was bred to hunt the European wild boars.

Wild boars are very fierce. They have long, sharp tusks. A tusk is a very long, curved tooth. Boars use their tusks like knives when they think they are in danger. They are fast and powerful. Hunters had a hard time getting close enough to wild boars to kill them.

Most dogs were no match for wild boars. The Germans bred a dog strong enough to fight with the dangerous boars. It had to be quick enough to escape from the fast-moving tusks.

The Germans crossed breeds to produce one of the largest dogs in the world. It had strong muscles but no extra weight. It had long legs to give it speed. It had large, powerful jaws. The Germans called it the Deutsche dogge. This means German mastiff in German.

# Chapter 3

# The Development of the Breed

By the 1700s, the German mastiff was hunting wild boars all across Europe. Italians simply called the dog alano. This is the Italian word for mastiff. For some reason, the French began calling them grand Danois. This means big Danish in French.

The English borrowed the French name. They translated grand Danois as Great Dane. The name stuck. In all English-speaking countries, the German mastiff is now called the great Dane. People in Germany and other parts of the world still call them German mastiffs.

**In Germany, Great Danes are called German mastiffs.**

## An Official Breed

In 1880, the first German mastiff or Great Dane club began in Germany. Interest in the breed spread quickly. A Great Dane club started in England in 1885. The Great Dane Club of America began in Chicago in 1889. It was the fourth breed club to join the American Kennel Club.

In 1891, the club in Germany wrote a description of what the ideal German mastiff or Great Dane should look like. This description has changed little over the years. It still describes what Great Dane fans are looking for in a dog.

**The description of the ideal Great Dane has changed little over the years.**

# *Chapter 4*

# The Great Dane Today

Today, Great Danes rarely hunt. They are still powerful and fast. But they are valued more for their beauty and spirit. They are one of the most loving dog breeds.

Great Danes do not live as long as some breeds. This is true of many large dogs. The average life of a Great Dane is just seven to ten years.

The American Kennel Club registers about 11,000 Great Danes every year. The Canadian Kennel Club registers about 700 per year.

**Great Danes are valued for their beauty and spirit.**

## Sizing Up the Great Dane

The most noticeable feature of the Great Dane is its size. Males stand 30 to 36 inches (76 to 91 centimeters) tall. Females stand 28 to 34 inches (71 to 86 centimeters) tall or higher. The height of a dog is measured from the ground to the withers. The withers are the tops of the shoulders.

Male Danes weigh 140 to 175 pounds (63 to 79 kilograms). Females weigh 110 to 140 pounds (49.5 to 63 kilograms). It takes one to three years for a Great Dane to reach its full height and weight.

The Great Dane has a long, curved tail. The tail is broader near the body. It comes to a point at the end. Its eyes are dark, and its nose is black.

**The Great Dane has a long, curved tail.**

## Ear Cropping

Dane puppies are born with medium-sized ears that fold down toward the cheek. Some people like to crop the ears. Crop means to cut a dog's ears so they come to a point at the top. This is done when the puppy is six or seven weeks old. The ears are then taped to make them stand up straight. When the ears heal, they stand up for the rest of the dog's life.

Ear cropping goes back to the days of hunting wild boars. The dog's ears were cropped so they would not be torn by a boar's sharp tusks. Long ears could also get completely ripped off in a fight.

Ear cropping is against the law in some European countries. It is not against the law in North America. More North American owners are questioning this practice. Still, almost all Danes competing in dog shows have cropped ears.

**Many Great Danes have their ears cropped and taped so they will stand up straight.**

**Great Danes may be harlequin-colored. Harlequin is white with black markings.**

## Dane Colors

Great Danes' coats come in at least eight colors. But only six are approved for breeding and dog shows. This means only dogs in one of the six colors can be shown. The approved colors are black, fawn, brindle, blue, harlequin, and mantle.

Fawn is golden tan with a black face. Brindle is gold with black, tigerlike stripes and a black face. Blue is a deep, steel gray. Harlequin is white with black markings all over the body except on the neck. Mantle is a black body with a white neck and front. The mantle color is sometimes called Boston coloring. This is because the color pattern is similar to the Boston terrier.

Danes can also be white or merle. Merle is speckled gray. Dogs of these colors are sometimes born to Harlequin-colored parents. White Danes are often deaf. Merles are usually healthy, but many merle-colored Danes have deaf or blind puppies. White and merle-colored Danes make fine pets, but they should not be used for breeding.

# Chapter 5

# Owning a Great Dane

Great Danes are good pets. They have gentle personalities. Danes make good watchdogs because they warn their families of strangers. But they are rarely mean.

Owning a Great Dane is a challenge because of its large size. A Dane puppy grows to about 100 times its birth weight in one year. Danes are expensive. They eat more food than other dogs. They need a larger bed or crate. Their health care costs more.

Because they are so big, Great Danes must be taught manners. They must never be allowed to jump on people. They could accidentally knock someone down.

Despite their size, Danes are good with children. They love to fight playfully, but they can knock children over just by licking them.

**Because they are such big dogs, Great Danes must be taught manners.**

## Keeping a Great Dane

Danes love to be with people. They do best living in a house with a family. Their short coats do not keep them very warm. They cannot stay outside in cold weather.

Many owners put dog sweaters or jackets on their Danes during walks in cold weather. Danes are not very active dogs. A long walk every day usually provides enough exercise.

Great Danes have long legs with large bones and not much fat. They can get calluses on their legs if they sleep on the floor. A callus is a hard patch of skin. Danes need something soft to lie on. This will help prevent painful calluses.

Dog owners need to make sure they can find their dog if it gets lost. Some people do this by putting their names and phone numbers on their dogs' collars.

Other owners have a microchip implanted under the dog's skin. A microchip is a computer chip about the size of a grain of rice. When scanned, it reveals the owner's name, address, and telephone number.

**A long walk every day usually provides a Great Dane with enough exercise.**

## Feeding a Great Dane

A good diet is important for Great Danes. They cannot eat all types of dog food. It is best to use a diet recommended by a veterinarian or an experienced Dane breeder. A veterinarian is a person trained and qualified to treat the sicknesses and injuries of animals.

Many Dane owners feed their dogs high-quality kibble. Kibble is dry dog food. Some owners moisten the food with water.

A full-grown Great Dane may eat more than two pounds (one kilogram) of kibble a day. A Dane should not be fed more than it needs. Danes must not be allowed to become overweight. It should be easy to see and feel the ribs on a healthy Great Dane.

## Wobbler's Syndrome

Wobbler's Syndrome is a spinal cord problem. The spinal cord is the part of the body that controls nerves and muscles. Wobbler's Syndrome is a condition that appears during the first year of some dogs' lives. Most dogs that have Wobbler's Syndrome are Great Danes.

**A good diet is important for a Great Dane.**

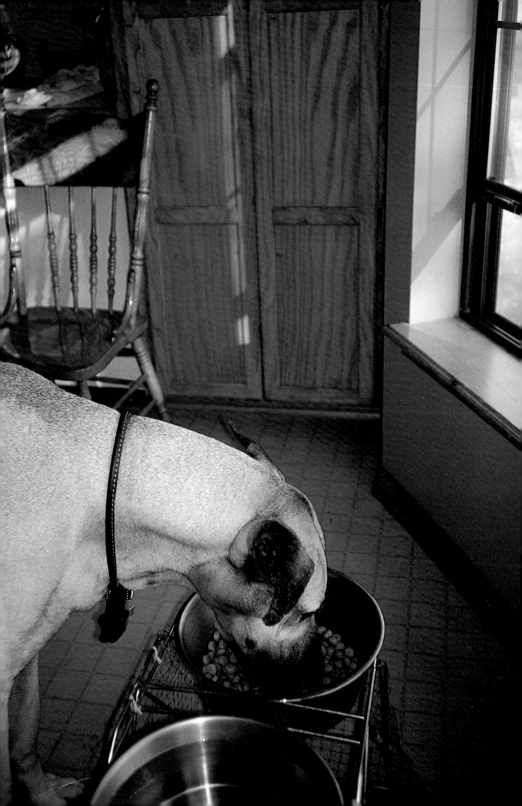

Puppies that have Wobbler's Syndrome seem fine at first. The problem usually shows up when puppies are between three months and one year old. The first sign is when the back legs fail to work properly.

The back legs will wobble or sway when dogs with Wobbler's Syndrome walk. The dogs may fall down often. They may drag their back feet. They might have trouble keeping their balance. As the disease becomes worse, the front legs also become affected.

Wobbler's Syndrome can be treated in many cases. Treatments include diet, drugs, special exercises, and surgery. If puppies are treated early enough, they may grow to be healthy adults.

## Canine Bloat

A Great Dane can develop a condition called canine bloat. Its stomach can move and get twisted. It fills with air and blocks the intestines. This condition can lead to death.

A dog that is bloated will appear anxious. It will not eat or drink. It may gag or vomit at first. Within half an hour to an hour, the

**Puppies with Wobbler's Syndrome can grow to be healthy adults.**

stomach will appear swollen. The dog will pant or breathe rapidly. The dog must be taken to a veterinarian immediately or it may die.

To help prevent canine bloat, a Dane should be fed small amounts often. Many owners feed their dogs two to four meals a day. A Dane should not be allowed to drink a large amount of water after eating.

A Dane should not exercise for at least half an hour before eating. It should not be walked for an hour and a half to two hours after eating.

## Grooming

Danes do not shed much. They do not need much grooming. Their coats should be brushed once a week. They should be bathed when needed. Some Great Danes drool.

A dog's toenails should be trimmed if they get too long. Its teeth and ears should be cleaned regularly. A veterinarian can show dog owners how to do these things.

**Great Danes do not need much grooming.**

## Health Care

Dogs need shots every year to protect them from serious sicknesses. They need pills to protect them from heartworms. A heartworm is a tiny worm carried by mosquitoes that enters a dog's heart and slowly destroys it. Dogs need checkups every year for all types of worms.

During warm weather, a dog should be checked for ticks. A tick is a small bug that sucks blood. Some ticks carry Lyme disease. This is a serious illness that can cripple an animal or a human. It should also be checked for fleas, lice, and mites. These are tiny insects that live on a dog's skin.

**Dogs should be checked for ticks, fleas, lice, and mites.**

## Finding a Great Dane

Too often, people buy Great Danes only to discover they cannot take care of them. Too many people buy cute puppies and forget they will grow into giant dogs. Some people do not realize how much it costs to feed a giant dog.

For these reasons, Great Danes are often available for adoption. Most of them are loving pets looking for a good home. Great Dane organizations have information about dogs that are available for adoption.

People wanting puppies should contact a Great Dane club to find a good breeder. Or they should ask a veterinarian to recommend one.

**Cute Great Dane puppies become giant adult dogs.**

**Tail**

**Hindquarters**

**Hock**

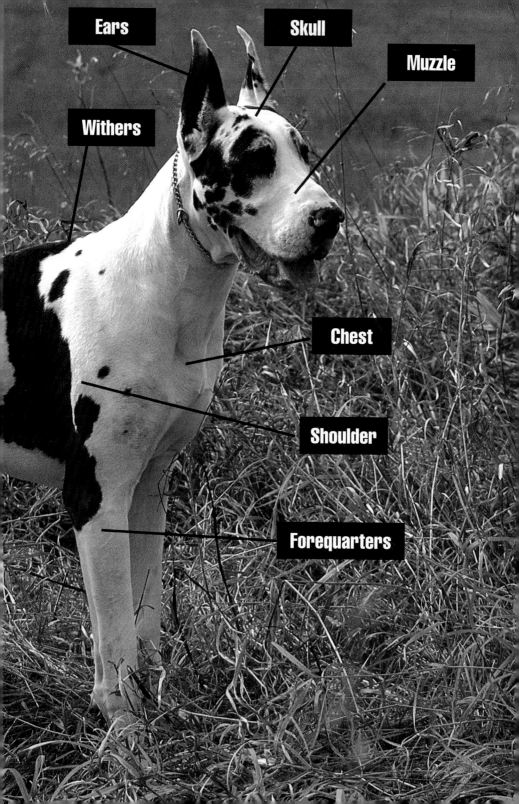

# Quick Facts about Dogs

## Dog Terms

A male dog is called a dog. A female dog is known as a bitch. A young dog is a puppy until it is one year old. A newborn puppy is a whelp until it no longer depends on its mother's milk. A family of puppies born at one time is called a litter.

## Life History

| | |
|---|---|
| Origin: | All dogs, wolves, coyotes, and dingoes descended from a single wolflike species. Dogs have been friends of humans since earliest times. |
| Types: | There are many colors, shapes, and sizes of dogs. Full-grown dogs weigh from two pounds (one kilogram) to more than 200 pounds (90 kilograms). They are from six inches (15 centimeters) to three feet (90 centimeters) tall. They can have thick hair or almost no hair, long or short legs, and many types of ears, faces, and tails. There are about 350 different dog breeds in the world. |
| Reproductive life: | Dogs mature at six to 18 months. Puppies are born two months after breeding. A female can have two litters per year. An average litter is three to six puppies, but litters of 15 or more are possible. |
| Development: | Puppies are born blind and deaf. Their ears and eyes open at one to two weeks. They try to walk at about two weeks. At three weeks, their teeth begin to come in. |

| Life span: | Dogs are fully grown at two years. If well cared for, they may live up to 15 years. |
| --- | --- |

## The Dog's Super Senses

| Smell: | Dogs have a sense of smell many times stronger than a human's. Dogs use their sensitive noses even more than their eyes and ears. They recognize people, animals, and objects just by smelling them. Sometimes they recognize them from long distances or for days afterward. |
| --- | --- |
| Hearing: | Dogs hear better than humans. Not only can dogs hear things from farther away, they can hear high-pitched sounds people cannot. |
| Sight: | Dogs are probably color-blind. Some scientists think dogs can see some colors. Others think dogs see everything in black and white. Dogs can see twice as wide around them as humans can because their eyes are on the sides of their heads. |
| Touch: | Dogs enjoy being petted more than almost any other animal. They can feel vibrations like an approaching train or an earthquake about to happen. |
| Taste: | Dogs do not taste much. This is partly because their sense of smell is so strong that it overpowers their taste. It is also because they swallow their food too quickly to taste it well. |
| Navigation: | Dogs can often find their way through crowded streets or across miles of wilderness without any guidance. This is a special dog ability that scientists do not fully understand. |

# Words to Know

**brindle** (BRIN-duhl)—gold with black tigerlike stripes and a black face

**callus** (KAL-uhss)—a hard patch of skin that can be painful

**heartworm** (HART-wurm)—a tiny worm carried by mosquitoes that enters a dog's heart and slowly destroys it

**kibble** (KIB-buhl)—dry dog food

**Lyme disease** (LIME duh-ZEEZ)—a disease carried by ticks that can cripple an animal or a human

**mastiff** (MASS-tiff)—in the past, any large dog used for hunting, herding, or fighting. Today, there are different breeds of mastiffs.

**merle** (MURL)—speckled gray

**microchip** (MYE-kroh-chip)—a computer chip about the size of a grain of rice, implanted under the skin to identify an animal

**register** (REJ-uh-stur)—to record a dog's breeding records with an official club

**veterinarian** (vet-ur-uh-NER-ee-uhn)—a person trained and qualified to treat the sicknesses and injuries of animals

**withers** (WITH-urs)—the tops of an animal's shoulders

# To Learn More

**Alderton, David**. *Dogs*. New York: Dorling Kindersley, 1993.

**American Kennel Club**. *The Complete Dog Book*. New York: Macmillan, 1992.

**Anderson, Brad**. *Marmaduke*. New York: Tor Books, 1991.

**Draper, Nancy-Carroll**. *The Great Dane, Dogdom's Apollo*. New York: Howell Book House, 1982.

**Nicholas, Anna Katherine**. *The Great Dane*. Neptune City, N.J.: T.F.H. Publications, 1988.

You can read articles about Great Danes in *AKC Gazette*, *Dane World*, *Dog Fancy*, *Dog World*, and *The Great Dane Reporter* magazines.

# Useful Addresses

**Association of Great Dane Fanciers**
Route 1
Milverton, ON N0K 1M0
Canada

**Great Dane Club of America**
1825 Oaklyn Drive
Green Lane, PA 18054

**Great Dane Club of Canada**
179 Harper Street
Winnipeg, MB R2J 1K4
Canada

**Great Dane Foundation**
3919 Wetmeadow
Houston, TX 77082

**Great Dane Rescue**
P.O. Box 5543
Plymouth, MI 48170

# Internet Sites

**Acme Pet**
http://www.acmepet.com

**American Kennel Club**
http://www.akc.org

**Great Dane Club of America**
http://www.users.cts.com/king/g/gdca/

**Marmaduke ®**
http://www.unitedmedia.com/comics/marmaduke/

# Index